Clichés
&
Other Pretty
Things

Olivia Nadine

<u>Dedication</u>

This book is dedicated to the dreamers still on the journey to reality and to my family who has supported me in all of my endeavors.

CONTENTS

Note from the Author

I have left the poems untitled.
Where you would find a traditional title, I have
left an open space for you to name your
interpretation of my expression.
I encourage you fill any blank pages as well.
I want this book, this experience, to be yours as
much as it is mine.

SECTION 1:

A Study In Life

1. _____

Insecurities in the mind
Lyrics on the paper
Flaws on parade
Scribbled into vapor
The proud & pompous know-it-all
Falls behind closed doors
The loud mouth diva
Releases the rudest snores
Things are rarely ever
Exactly what they seem
She may look broke down and worthless
But truly is a queen
To be loved and respected
The misunderstood, the "brotha" from the hood
Born in the mean streets of Palm Springs
Had to rough it with two loving parents
An older brother and a younger sister
Hard Knock life on the swings
The CEO in the benz
Once just the trailer park king
Flipping burgers before night school
Just to make ends
Saved up money for college
Ended up with a full ride
Don't try to bring him down
Because he has pride
Everyone has a story
Never are they all the same
From good to bad, or worse to better
We all have stories
To share together

2. _____

Have life before death
Friends over foes
Laughter to tears
And dreams not deferred

Let time be well spent
Things happily done
Joy exuding through
Work and fun

Let the light not only
Shine in the day
Blind darkness
So it never stands in the way

Give life a chance
To blossom and bloom
Give death a break
And give yourself some room

Life is for the living
The loving and learning can have it too
But from where I stand
It seems like death best fits you.

3. _____

Everything don't look right on every body
Or on everyone
Some words are grammatically incorrect
But they still get the job done
Like saying don't
When it should be doesn't
Or dissing your cousin
While playing the dozens
Depending on your audience
You might speak
With words that cause suspense

Or wear your platinum suspenders
Of the great pretender
Camouflaged for the battle of life
But in the wrong suit
You'll miss the flight
Pulled aside to get checked out
While the bomber walks
All decked out
In the latest attire
Stand aside, the man's on fire
Burning with curiosity
The same thing that killed the kitty

But of course you knew all that
That's why you're big boned not fat
And you love the song baby got back
Because baby that's all you have
A back, and a half
Well that and being great at math

Every calculus test you did pass

But people never get to that
Because they can't get over
That outfit that should have stayed on the rack
The one that takes away from your brain
While showing all your back- and a half
Reducing your intelligence
To the length of your spandex

You cry that it is unfair
And I won't say that isn't true
But darling, that outfit still doesn't fit you

4. _____

The surprise of a new sunrise
Should remain as such
No day is guaranteed
May never have another lunch
Hunger or death
One second one breath
Differences can be made
Change created and erased
Time is not under man's control
We cannot dictate how it flows
Seconds are fleeting
Especially in weeping
Minutes are joyous
In proud parents eyes
Days are a lifetime
When dreams come true
In a year there is no limit
To the good, bad, and ugly
Just one person can do
If a drop of rain can tip the scale
A drop of blood
Can bring heaven or hell
Life and breath
Reaching in to the everlasting
Grasp the intangible
Only to find the instability
That makes the temporary so sweet

5. _____

Standing in the world alone
No place to call a home
He looks left and right
Crossing the street
Based on faith not sight
Reciting prayers and lines
Deep into the night
Morning prayer to start the day
Venturing into a world
No one, yet, knows his name
Choosing whether or not to play their game
Is it fame he's after?
Or just a young child's laughter?
The delight in a little girl's eye
The joy of inspiring cheers and tears
At the end of the day
It wasn't a performance
As much as a form of treatment
Taking the pain out of a young boy's eyes
Replacing hurt with joy
In the young lives
Provide an escape
A chance to getaway
Even if just for a moment of time
The burdens of their world become like air
Giving them a chance to dance on a cloud
Love of the craft and the laugh of a child

6. _____

Live life systematically random
And oh the things that will happen
The fun to be had
Laughs to be made

Time will past
Such a joy to create
Through random acts of life
Kindness and joy overshadow
The lamenting pain

Live life purposefully
Becoming who you ought to be

Make a way through the mountain
Place a bridge over the sea

Embrace life and its
Systematic Randomousity

7. _____

Abstract minds think in abstract time
Be it not wasted
The sweet days untasted
The mantra on my heels
The devil tried to make a deal
But I made one with God instead
He held my hand and lifted up my head
Abstractions are creative input
The distractions from idle hands
Then out intriguing words in the air
From mouth they did appear
The lines of the brush
Become flushed with rush
The night silence is hushed
Pass the pulpits and ditches
The speakers stand on both sides
Colorful world full of mystical creatures
The Street corner preacher
And the back alley rapper
The superhero mother
The Multi-faceted father teacher
The dedicated pupils of students
Stare and absorb
The mind expands like sponges
Untouched by a sword
The pen is their weapon
It stops the foes
For the greatest imagination
Opens both concrete and abstract doors

8. _____

To the girl who thinks
Her biggest assets
Are her ass & tits
She needs to recognize
That she has a mind
And she must nurture it

Her possibilities become limitless
As they multiply
Faster than her legs divide
Her scars will disappear
As if they never lived
Because her body
No longer holds her head high
No one part
Be it breasts, lips, or thighs
Will be the defining characteristic
Instead intellect will push it

Knowledge to life
Above flesh
To a new level of self confidence
That's says it's okay to live fully
And to live up to your potential
Beyond your 34-26-36 measurements

9. _____

Be it to me and not to you
My opinion of me
Has more value than
Your restrictions
In a world of contradictions
Preaching free love
While fostering hate
Plastic surgery
So you can love your face
Disgraceful behavior
From those with holy favor
When really it's just
Holy flavor
Because they never
Truly caught the spirit
But, no, you don't want to hear it
Because you'll do you
And I'll do me
But that's not the way
It's supposed to be
Checks and Balances
Rights and Wrong
A sin is a sin even if put to a song
So who are we to judge?
You say everyone
I say no one
Only he who is blameless
Can cast the first stone

10. _____

The arrogant and the ignorant
Run ramped in the world
They come in many shapes and forms
Man, woman, boy, or girl
No matter the face
Or the way they speak
Listen not to their truths
For it only deceives
The dance of the closed eyes
Shouts of deaf minds
From breath to death
The ignorant don't know
Or at least so they say
The Arrogant know it all
Or so they often complain
But the worse of the two
A combination of the unideal
The useless Ignorant Arrogant
The proud unknowing
The stubborn vacancy
Time after time
The ideals they created
The ones that no one believes
They hold fast
And claim a flag
For the world of them
Forgetting you can't make up the truth
Refusing to recognize the life of those with
Open eyes
The reality of me and you

11. _____

She knows it all
The world is nothing new
Been there done that
Seen the first and last
But she knows nothing
The vast vapid expanse
Of her over confidence
Is like knowledge filling a bottomless bucket
Riddled with holes and filled with sand
If untouched
It seems to weight too much
Too vast to grasp
But upon examination
And shallow contemplation
The truth is exposed
As are the holes
The knowledge is of the less than substantial
The non-monumental
The experiences of a half lived life
But knowledge she says
And thus thinks she has
A truth that only resides within her head
Because she still knows nothing
Henceforth creating knowledge that is dead.

12. _____

Who died last died best
Be them one or many
A he or she
Survival of the fittest
For we survived
Only to perish
But those few extra moments
We eternally cherish
For we were blissful at last
Those silent moments
After you had passed
Others don't know our woe
The times you came
When you'd never go
The brutality you caused
Much devastation you brought
The lives you took
For the times hard fought
So your passing brings sweet release
Life given to the soon deceased

13. _____

She stood over top
Looking down on her youth
Like only a wise mother could
She scrutinized her size
The curl pattern and hair height
Stand tall
Back straight
Flowed as constant as
Good morning
Aesthetics are the display
Of one's intelligence
A daily lesson
She never missed
A slurred diction
Denoted sloppy continence
Goodness forbid
The appearance of an untucked shirt
A sign of disregard
And utter disrespect
Each step ought to be deliberate
The path we walk
Cannot be riddled with hesitation
One's head should be held high
For if your eyes are forward
Your direction is too
Molded by the constant reminders
The youth becomes a lady
The boy transforms to man
Childhood lessons
And positive progress
Go hand in hand

SECTION 2:

Variations in Love

14. _____

what is love
i cannot quantify it
or trap it with science

sometimes it cannot be seen, heard, or felt
but its presence is there

is it love that calls me back to you
years after departure

or masochistic tendencies
that make me weep

i think i love you
but find me and kiss me once more
so that i can know for sure

15. _____

Don't search for what you can't see
You'll end up grasping for all eternity
What you find would never be
Just disoriented dreams
Manufactured and store brought
The poster on every wall
But still the prize will allude you
Gone spring come fall

The temporary fixes
Haze your golden eyes
Numb to the truth
When the haze is gone
So is your treasure
Because your couldn't wait
Indulged in instant pleasure
Never high measure
Cheap quality high quantity

Filled with remorse and regret
Still searching for the intangible
Love and happiness

16. _____

I want a guy whose arms
become a second home
Whose laugh is infectious
Spreading joy through my bones
I want a love destined by God
And discovered in the depths of my heart
Where a pre-nup is not a thought
And neither is being apart
Where our dreams are equal if not the same
I want a love who is my umbrella in the rain
But when winter comes I can be his cover
Day and night I search for this phantom lover
Maybe not actively
And a little too passively
But search for him I do
In my mind I always ask
Is it you? Is it you?
Knowing that one day it'll
Come true
On its own, when I least expect it
Because I can't find you until
I can live without you
I won't see you until
I don't need you
So then I begin to wonder
If & when we'll ever meet
Because it's hard to function
When you're missing a critical piece

17. _____

The light of your eyes
Is the sun in my sky
Don't turn away
From me now
Don't blind me
With the darkness
Of your absence
I crave your presence
Its luminescence
This little light of mine
Shine baby shine

18. _____

The aroma of your aura
So sweet to me
Drawn to you like honey
Traps a bee
The nectar of you neck line
A delicious treat
Oh you're a sweet, sweet treat
Yes indeed

19. _____

Secrets, lies and deception
Breached the surface
Crept onto her face
She couldn't hide the truth

It found its way out
She couldn't stop it
And she didn't try to
He had to find out

He had to know why
Why she was distant, frantic and confused
So scared of being used and abused
When all he did was love her
Time and time again

She let it all out
And he just took it all in
For hours it came
Like a raging river
So many things
Secrets he didn't know
And couldn't imagine

But she had to tell them
He had to know
He sat there absorbing

So much that it took most of the night
When it was over
She prepared for a fight
But instead, he sat
Silent and still
Minutes turned to hours

He didn't speak,
Just looked
Confused she stood
Prepared for anything but this

Especially the first words
That came out of his lips

I still love you, flaws and all,
I always have and always will
I just hope you'll have me still

20. _____

Sing a song for me
One with a beautiful harmony

Sing for me

Say how you truly feel
Tell me something new

True and real

Sing a song for me
About every possibility
Tell me about who you are
And who you wish to be
Tell me something I don't know

Will you sing it to me?

Music makes depth disappear
Takes a cloudy truth
Makes it crystal clear
There are so many things I want to hear

Will you sing them to me dear?

21. _____

Speechless she stands
Resisting the urge
To grab, take
Hold your hand
Step back not closer
She runs
But there is no escape
The pain
The joy
The future looks brightly grim
Bright for the prospects
Grim without you
But she thinks
Hard
She knows what she must do
Live life
No matter the pain
Live life
Through a sea of tears
Live life
For endless years
Live life
And live it as her own
So live she does
But speechless she loved

22. _____

Wait. Write.
Breathe.
I can't speak
Write
I can't love
Like
But I love to like and I like to love
But I don't want to go against the one above
But what if I'm going with and not against
But what if buts don't exist
When I love
I love to love
And I love you
But I can't say it so
Wait. Breathe.
Write.
How do I hide it
It burst from inside me
Everything I try to do
It overrides me
Divides me
As the butterflies multiply
Hide oh Lord
I lie in wait for a sign
For I can't speak therefore I write
I lie in wait for a word from you
Wait. Breathe.
Write.

23. _____

It's not hard for me
To say what's on my mind
But what's in my heart
Tears me apart
The doubt and anxiety
Divide and conspire against me
Intellectual controversies
Dealt with eloquence and sophistication
But when it comes to emotions
It's a more delicate persuasion
Blunt words
Become ones of evasion
Never able to clearly say
What I dream about at night
And ponder on during the day
This porcelain container
Has tremendous capacity
But also falls with alarming frequency
So when I say I love you
Know that it took me a while
I had to verify
That it was more than just gravity
And realer than fantasy
My heart is much too shy to lie
But my brain can't bear to pick up
Shattered pieces again
So excuse my timid-ness
Chalk it up to innocence
And keep my heart safe
For it is delicate

24. _____

Someday
Somehow
These feelings
Will arrive with less frequency
One day
I won't think of you
Won't wish for what could be
Just love and enjoy what is
Because a life based on
The imagination of fantasy
Dulls a once bright reality
Wishing I was the one for you
Knowing I can live without you
Not that I wanted to
Mentally I'm selfish
Physically restless
Hoping this is just a test
Reality says otherwise
And I often listen
Only side tracked
When dreams glisten in a dreary sun
Only on the quiet days
Can I hear my heart
Try to block it out
Avoid falling apart
Someday
Sometimes

25. _____

I wrote you a poem

But you'll probably never see it

Or any of them

Not until I'm ready

Until I'm strong and brave

Until that day

Just know

I wrote a poem

Filled with raw truths

Unspoken

And I wrote it for you

26. _____

[Part I]
Don't lose the piece of my heart
I gave it to you shaped as a rock
But my quick mind and fragile heart
Were slow to know
I try to forget
Let go
Be free

But something I can't remove
Brings me back to you
I can't stop my thoughts
From rushing in your direction
Your face flashes in my mind like an hour chime
But I have a notion
That we will never be
And the truth is
I am afraid to never know
To grow old with regret
Me as its bitter mistress

I'm afraid that I love you
And you don't love me back
I'm afraid that I can't stop thinking about you
Knowing that I never want to stop
My heart broke at the thought of you
So lost in emotions crying was all I could do
But yet I still long for you more
I prayed and pleaded
Never once believing
You and I could become we

Telling myself from day one
It wasn't meant to be
But if it's not meant to be then
Why does my heart ache?

My skins tingles at your proximity
Awakens with sensitivity at a mere brush past me
I don't trust myself alone with you
Knowing that everything I wanted
I would never do
Because your friendship is too precious to lose
To be together may be a dream come true

But then what of my dreams before I met you
I want to travel the world and be successful in
my own right
Can a relationship be over the phone?
Would it cause me to pause and savor the
precious moments alone
Or would it all be too much to bear
I want you to reach out and tell me
"We'll worry about it when we get there"
I want the guarantee of you standing next to me
To be able to tell you everything I feel inside
Knowing that I am not alone
That together replaces on my own.

So, I gave you a piece of my heart
And dipped it in a rock
So that you couldn't break it
And it wouldn't be torn apart
Though I tried to give you a tiny piece
You snatched my breath away from me

27. _____

[Part II]
If I was courageous I would call you
Connect with you day and night
But my fear of rejection
Makes me take pause at my reflection
And wonder why this was given to me

Did I manifest emotions?
Is this real?
Or am I stuck in my head?

I want to be free of wondering
Without the burden of releasing the truth
I want to call you and tell you everything

I got sad that you were leaving
Scared you would never come back
To be always near that was my selfish request

But I couldn't tell you the truth
The truth that you already knew
The cowardice in me won't allow me to tell you a
known truth

Will saying it set me free or cause more agony
Of an undesired reality
Tainted with resurgent fantasy

I'm only fooling myself to
Think that I'm keeping a secret
I'm simply just avoiding the truth

You already know I love you
And I don't know how you feel about me
I could analyze past conversations
Hoping to come to a grand revelation
That says I'm free to ask you
Because the answer is guaranteed

But love
Doesn't really depend on rationale
Or mere persuasion
So, instead I gave you my heart

Shrunken down into a rock. I just kept a piece for
myself
So that when you threw it out there would still be
something left

And I could regain my breath

28. _____

Love is my inspiration

My desperation comes from its depletion
My elation from its proximity
Well-being because it's my remedy

Love is motivation
My laughter in the spring
Hugs in the summer
Warmth in the winter
Comfort through the fall

It is my year-round joy
Live a life full of love
From the earth below
To the heavens above

Love is the one thing of which
There is never enough

SECTION 3:

Strictly Non²sense

29. _____

It's time
For some nonsense rhymes
The ones that always
Drop a dime
Often seem like a waste
Of time
Like lemon lime
On a bright summer day
Trying not to melt away
Fun! please stay
Forever
Always
Nonsense doggerel
You wish you knew me very well
Wishes no spells
Just Kisses
Can't you tell
It's early
Wishing it was late
The greatness of the moment
Is bait for the future
Lure your mind
Waste of time
Your time to be exact
But that's opinion
Not a fact
Because if you enjoyed this
Then I am remiss
To admit
That I had fun writing this
Complete and utter
Nonsense

30. _____

And now the Adventures

Of Samantha Venture!

Just another day for the little girl

Another chance to explore the world

She'd been to the moon

And back again

She's studied the rocks

And how they turn to sand

But today was special

Different from them all

Today Samantha Venture

Is going to the Mall

But not just any mall

The largest one of all

With things to see

And places to go

People to meet, well you know

From day start till end

She ventured to her heart's content

And ended the day relaxing

Sitting with Ol' Abe Lincoln

31. _____

Sunshine and quiet rhymes
The sublime lines
Rest on a tablet
Written in a stone soul
A hot heart brings the
Forgotten back to life

The curve things
Become straight
But not necessarily right
The passion is there
The weather is fair
The long flowing hair
But then nonsense obstructs the view
The paradise
Over the hill still waits
Only for you, no other may enter

Freezing winters occur
Hour after hour
The disaster struck
Whipping back and forth
The ups and downs of life
Strike hard
But the joys heal better
Sunshine and quiet skies
Complimentary fair weather

32. _____

Silly saying Silly thoughts
Not as stupid as I once brought
Just a different way of expressing
What others won't be professing
Excuse me ma'am for my faux pas
I do not know what happened
On my free style wig
Split it open only to find
Too much commotion
Like the ocean
Leaping wide and wild
Not to be subdued
Much like a stuck up child
My mind will have its way
And its own days
So hear me first
When I scream it loud
I refuse to be one of the crowd
Be it my dialogue
Or my costume dress
Nothing less than what I suspect
If I don't like it, I flip it
If it conflicts, I strip it
Exploring its twisted depth
Looking until there is nothing left
Unknown or unseen
Exploration through the seams
Of your reality and my fantasy
Perception of intersection
The cross play on our mind games
Lost in the pontification of my imagination
Silly sayings & deep thoughts

33. _____

Something…something rather
Deep
…Yeah deep, that's the word

Something rather deep crept up
…hmm like winter sunrises?
In my mind and out my eyes?
The second one, yeah that one

So something deep crept
No wait, wait
What I meant to say…

Something rather deep crept up
Inside of me until it is was out
Upright before my eyes
The lies my mother told
Became age old truths
Ruthlessly devouring what is left of me

Mentally and physically?
Ritualistically? Calisthenics?
I think I need a medic
To clear the debris
Shrapnel still left
After last week
Fire fights silenced

The meek and well intentioned
The collision could have been avoided
But the damage not undone

I still collapse every time I try to run

But my past is still behind me
Flagging each side of me
Living becomes devoid of fun
Like a light without love
There is a sparkling void
A sun fallen below from above
Into the depths of a shallow mind
Heatless creep of a winter sunrise
Rise and yet I fall

Deep, yeah, deep

34. _____

Ink pens and space ships
Spray paint and Lipstick
All make bold statements

Exploration
And division
Subtraction and creativity

Never mind the tool
Just the masterpiece
A piece of a master
Their heart and mind
A little soul spread thin
Just for a dime

Time is money
So they work fast
Quick rhymes
And a swift brush
Lil blush and a hush

The art work incomplete
The weeks
Turn dark at night
The daylight
Always in constant flight

The right and the wrongs of the world
Put on a canvas
For every little boy and girl
And even those in between

A nightmare and a dream
The world needs a word
But gets a painting instead
That says more than a sentence ever said

The nights become welcoming
And the days a warm shelter
The masterpiece did its job
Can't get one better

35. _____

Marathon of Weird

Dreams played in my

Heading out the door

Stepping in to the fresh

Air raids on my

Imagination's destination

Suspending time and

Space out and about

The house rock

Dropped socks

And kicking rocks

But don't stop the

Music moves me and let the

Groove find you

Dreamland ran by the Sandman

36. _____

Sublime mango creates a tango
The tongue dances its bud romance
The drama of juice
The lava and its ooze
Times become twisted
Wish list dipped into fantasy
Laced with reality
Construed to privacy
Step behind closed eyes
To see a mango tango fantasy

37. _____

Silence rambles on through the night
Not stirring a creature, or making a fright
Tripping slowly
Crashing softly
Lofty hopes and dreams
Gone with the way of light
Deep into the silent night

38. _____

It's time again
To hear your favorite girl
And her many adventures
Around the world
Samantha Venture is her name
Exploring the world is her game
Today is a new chance
To see the world
So let's get ready
To follow your girl!
Today's adventure started right here
In the hidden jungle in the air
Samantha found a ladder earlier today
And being her, she just climbed away
Didn't really know where it was going
All she knew is she was going too
The rope was long
It went way up high
Venture looked up and almost touched the sky
The birds were below her
The clouds above
She climbed that rope
Until she felt a tug
She came to a cloud
So large and dense
It made a shadow on the world that
Hasn't been seen since
Well she went right through that cloud she did
And when she got though,
She was sure glad she did
There were plants and animals out of this world
Everything to bring a smile

To any boy or girl
Venture roamed and wandered through the woods
In the jungle, and even the hood
All so pleasant, and a joy to see
Around one corner were bricks of gold
On the other side beaches that never got cold
Laughter and joy ripe for the picking
Honey comb so sweet
It was finger licking
Hour after hour
She found a little more
Still Venture got tired
She found a bed and rested till four
She woke up refreshed wanting more
But when she looked around
Nothing the same did she see
All she saw was her room staring back casually.
She went to the closet to look for the rope
But there were just her clothes
She looked outside for the cloud so dense
But all she saw was a clear blue sky and white
picket fence
On her leg she felt something dripping
She reached in her pockets
To find honey comb
Oh so finger licking
She closed her eyes and laughed and laughed
Drifting off to sleep
Back to the fun she just had

39. _____

Yawn

Tired sets in

Stretch

The process begins

Yawn

Unwinding and undermining

My ....

Yawn

Sleep consuming

The end is looming

The night grows darker

But not close enough

Hrmph

Standing becomes tough

Sit for a little while

..ZZZZZZZZZZZZ

Oh dear excuse me

While…

I…

Sleep……..

SECTION 4:

Into the Spirit

40. _____

Confessions of a sinner

Confessions of me

Confessions of a liar

Not who I am supposed to be

Confessions of a fake

The façade of the mirror

Confessions of a female

Tired of the role

Confessions of a person

Many mistakes to total

Confessions of me

To maybe help the troubles of you

41. _____

I need someone to talk to
Someone to listen to all of my problems
Soothe my fears
And at the same time talk of the future
Be it seconds or years.
To plan a life
Establish rivers of change
To float free from societal chains
I know I have that person in God,
                              But can I talk to the God in you?

42. _____

Sometimes it's the small touch
A simple gesture
That sparks hope
And inspires joy
Let not the small
Become insignificant
For a seed is small
Before bringing forth
A mighty tree
You may never know
Just how great
A small touch of love
Can be

43. _____

Addiction to affliction
My being becomes a contradiction
Such sin penetrates my mind
While I try to be holy
Claiming to only seek the divine
A contradiction and a hypocrite
I cannot stomach it
Constantly I repent
I constantly give in
Is there any hope or mercy left for me
Not like there deserves to be
All I ever seem to do is betray
Betray myself and my beliefs

For what?
Temporary satisfaction
Followed by grief, guilt, and anger after
I'm not ignorant
I know my sin
Each time I commit
I know what I'm doing
I know I shouldn't
Could say I don't want it
That wouldn't be the complete truth
So instead I say
Father forgive me for I have sinned
Again
Today

44. _____

Lying here at night

Staring into the light

Outside my window calls

I reach beside me

But it's not there

Check the other side

And there it hides

I open to the familiar page

The words soothe me

My worries go away

As my head falls, rest rises

And it's ok because

"I lie down and sleep;

I wake again, because the Lord sustains me"

Psalm 3:5 (NIV)

45. _____

Walking down the street
Singing for all to hear
And none to see
You heard my song
My melodic cry
A crescendo of tears
Soothed me from days to years
In my restless anticipation
Of things yet to come
Helped me slow down
And appreciate moments of life
Planning for the future
Is only good
If the present is understood
Now I think twice
Of your reaction to my actions
Seeking first your satisfaction
Because after years of trying
I finally feel like I'm starting to get it right
I'm seeing things
Before invisible to me
Like how your love surrounds me
Many forms and facets
Shepard this lamb
Help me stand when I am weak
Speak when I am mute
Lord your presence I cannot refute
My life is in your hands

46. _____

Laughter is tremble
And joy is the bass
Content is the melody
And love is a harmony
Life is the singer
Never knowing the genre to choose
And we,
Well, we are the writers
Of the concert's songs
With notes both right & wrong
Though ultimately that's up to the conductor
He directs the concert
The song order and arrangement
Though we exercise the power
To rearrange it
We may think that the selection
Won't flow
Or that these notes won't go
So we take matters into our own hands
And see the outcome and result
Take on the cacophony of consequences
We say we'll let him run the next production
Eventually we give up
And run it he does
It is only then that we get any applause

47. _____

Yesterday wasn't easy
Neither was the night before
Many times I cried
Tried not to hit the floor
But when I am weak
He is strong
He keeps my safe
In loving arms
Though I cried through the night
The morning saw drier eyes

48. _____

When she died I cried
But then joy dried my eyes
I thought of all the good memories
The laughs and the hugs
The real and true love
And I was no longer sad
We enjoyed the time we had
Didn't think it would end this soon
Or in such a way
But we all have our day
Her memories were a comfort
Jesus saving her was a joy
Her life was a blessing
So why cry when I'll see her once more

49. _____

There's a change a coming
A rain to wash away the imperfections
A snow to cleanse the air
Strong winds will blow
But will you still stand?
Or become like grains of sand
Gone with the wind
Lacking a foundation
Gone, like so many nations
One with history
Simply because you cease to be
Find your foundation
Your strong hold
The warmth in the cold
Where your name
They know
For storms will rage
Change will roll
But those grounded in faith
Though surrounded with turmoil
Will emerge unscathed
Transformed from the before
Improved in the after
To take on the unsurmountable
With Joy
Strength
And Laughter

50. _____

Soothing sounds
A calming melody
Course and surge straight through me
Smoothing frazzled ends
Making rough edges
Smooth
This tired soul
Fresh.
Renewed.
Marvel at what
The Gospel can do

51. _____

Silence in the room
Chaos invades the world
Light leaks from the box
Darkness spreads, never stops
Threatens to smother
Hope in the light
In a box in a silent room
Lost in a world
Which has lost its way

Hope sits waiting....

SECTION 5:

The Struggle

52. _____

The pain of lost runs deep
My heart aches with each pop
A future dies on every city block
Stunted by obsolete knowledge
Degraded with oppressive imagery
A constant theft of dignity
Lost hope
Stolen promise
Dashed prospects
Words of blood & pictures of distress
Dark realities cuts deep through the illusion of
progress
Assessments of success fall short
When measured against
The depths of loss on the concrete
Stone faces blink blind eyes
Fixated on a manufactured prize
Urban sprawl mirage
Unmoved by the river
As loss life flows over their feet
Dead hearts stare ahead
Focused on dreams deaf with beats
But my humanity
Pulls me to my knees
Overcome by the loss
I weep & weep

53. _____

Does your mind control your body?
Or is it the other way around?
How do you respond
At the smell of such delectable treats
Makes your mouth water
To succumb to it
Or manage to maintain order
Fall slave to the desire
Temptation is waiting on the fryer
Or do you say no
There something better waiting at home
Training your body
By telling it yes and no
Which one has the stronger will power?
The question becomes more daunting
Hour by the hour
Mind over body
Body over mind

54. _____

She sits
Quiet
Hours past
Drip
The cold has settled over
Numb
Down to her bones
Drip
The silence is deafening
Tock
Thoughts tick away like seconds
Quiet she sits
Numb she lives
Such a waste
She has so much to give
Numb to humanity
Lost sensibility

55. _____

Parasitic devotion
Feeding off your presence
Giving nothing back
Constantly taking
Tit & tat
And you always have more
More than I ever could
But I wish I would
For others to feed off me
Not I on thee
So I say to me
Set me free
That I may live separately

56. _____

Hidden deep inside
A creature unseen
Brilliant and Beautiful
But outside she sits
Obedient and dutiful
Never satisfied with life
Not able to turn left or right
Not able to sleep through the night
Night terrors plague her
Storm clouds rage within
She looks for a friend
Someone to hold her hand
But there is no one to take
Such a burden for a volunteer position
Because they can't see the instant reward
Love and joy they hoard
Though there's more than enough
More than enough
More than enough to go around
So she sits
Quiet and Obedient
Constantly subservient
Withering
Waiting. Waiting. Waiting.
Never the knights only the nots

57. _____

She sits

Silent

Forced into confinement

Into a contraption of her own making

A shell only she can break

Or her life it will take

She sits silent

Relentlessly trying to live

Receiving just so she can give

But they take too much

She has so little left

She gave her love

Repaid in anger

She gave her joy

Returned with strife

She gave them everything

Blindly, they took her life

As she sat

Silent

58. _____

Refresh Refresh
To be fresh again
To rejuvenate within
Refresh Refresh
It doesn't work
Refresh Refresh
Not connected to a network
Seek and Find
Seek and Find
Search my phone
Search my mind
No Signal no service
No open networks near
Blocked and Rejected
Dejected & let down
Refresh Refresh
Tear to Ground

59. _____

Kill the noise
Dislodge the distractions that divide my attractions
Kill the noise
Silence the sensation that deliver temptation
Kill the noise
Eliminate the extra the superficial
Kill the noise
Destroy the dictations of disaster
Kill the noise
Stifle the sounds that drive the mind mad
Happy fled and sad saw vacancy
Brought the whole posse
Depression, anguish, & angst oh my
The noise they bring clouds my head
With booming voices of dreams turned dead
Kill the noise that says no
Kill the noise that says stop
Kill the noise that says failure
Kill the noise that says defeat
Stomp it down with your own beat
Kill the noise that say disaster,
Won't ever turn it around
I'm the DJ so I'll decide how the track sounds
Turn the noise into music
Depression into dance
Kill all the noise that says I can't
Kill the noise inside my head

SECTION 6:

Claiming Victory

60. _____

Once a month, I choke

My throat swells and closes

My breath quickens, heart sinks

Blinking away invisible tears

My eyes can't focus

My choking and drowning,

Suffocating on my own insignificance,

Crushed by my inaction and

Paralyzed by my apathy

Some get cramps

Others are blessed to bloat

A chocolate binge is enough for others

But no

Mother Nature graced me with introspection

& a burden for greatness

And once a month

The burden becomes tangible

Unmistakably physical

And yet, I sit, unmoved

I think without taking action

Dream without daring initiations

Plans, preparation, and yet unmoved

I choke

I choke on what could have been

What could yet be

& on failure

Looming futures

Dreams like raisins

And feet like stones

They choke me

And I will continue to be choked,

To be paralyzed and halted

Until I remove my hands from around my neck

Take a deep breath

Pray to God for strength

And walking to the light of grace and my potential

And out of the darkness of fear

Maybe next month I'll breathe

Or at least choke less

61. _____

Stop.

Drop what you're doing

And just

SCREAM

Scream away your frustration

Shout your dreams

Yell what you've been holding back

Express your feelings

Let loose of the baggage

Break free of the chains

Yesterday was the last day.

Scream till it hurts less

Today is something new.

Sing till it feels better

Dance away the pain

Enjoy sunshine and rain

Yesterday is over and

Tomorrow has yet to come

But today,

Today is here

Make it yours

& Scream

62. _____

To freestyle

Is to flow without bounds

Let your mind run free

For nobody and everyone

Your individuality

Is a simple melody

Problems a marching beat

Treading under your feet

The circumstance is an audience

Reflecting the reaction

And substance of your determination

Turn your frustration

Into verbal elation

Contemplations become musical sensations

It's what you feel

And what you hear

From a flow so free

Liberating the broken down

Lifting and releasing

Stress decreasing

The unrestricted flow

A style all you

Freedom in reach

Enhanced by dope beats

73

63. _____

Odd balls of the world
Stand up
Let them know
You. Are. Here.

The counter culture
To the sub standards
Deviants from anchored
Prestige that runs like a disease
Making clones and drones
To follow the queen bee of society

Goes buzz in your ears
Stinging your eyes
Making little one's cry
Tormented by their imperfections
Not knowing perfect is just another way
To say the best you
The best me
The best unique individual you can be

But no

But people never seem to get quick
To their tricks

So odd balls of the world stand up
Step outside the box
Stay clever and creative
Maybe even a little outrageous

Whatever they say
It won't faze us
Because in the end they'll be like dust
Large in number but under our feet
As we stand and walk to our own beat

Odd balls, appreciate & create
That which is great

64. _____

Immaculate
A state of utter clean
Not me or my regime
The life I live
Is blemished at best
But still I try
Facing every test
The trials of life
Never easy, always hard
Never undoable
Always reaching for the stars
The light of the smile
Lights hundreds of miles
The beam of an eye
Like a search light in the night sky
Reach high pass the past
Into the future
What was does influence what is
But does not determine what can be
For him or her
For You and me
So Live
No matter the struggle
Live
Continuously
Live
With all boldness
Find what you seek
Fulfill your brilliant destiny

65. _____

The story must be told
No regrets for old
Age is just a number
Not a hindrance
Or a creator of belligerence
Life gives what you put in it
So I put in my all
Even if I fall
Hit the ground, unable to get up
I won't give up
Because there is always a way
Each day gives something new
Innovation lies within you
Seek within yourself
Not everyone else
Like the teachers used to say
Ask three before me
Ask yourself before he or she
Because if they can tell you
More about you than thee
Something is.....
Wrong is not a strong enough word
Your own words, have you not heard?
Or do you block them out with
Rhythm and Beat
The addictive sounds of the street
Or blind them out with UV lights
Never trusting your own sights
Walking blind with neither faith nor sight
Trust
Your story counts too
And no one can tell it better than you

66. _____

Sing a song true and loud
Let it reach unto the clouds
Do a dance strong and free
Let it have no boundaries
Make a painting bright and bold
Something timeless
Of present & stories untold
Compose a poem deep and rich
Suspend time and make a wish
Let the forever know
You were here
And have something to say
May it go down in history
Not textbooks, galleries or museums
But forever in the hearts of those near
Those few who opened
Their eyes and ears
And heard light come alive
Let your expression traverse
Time and space
No one shall be able to contain it
In a small constricting box
For once your expression is free
It is in its purest form
And has infinite possibilities
So let go and live free
Let the world know you were here

67. _____

Sing your song

That song you sing so well

That song that is your own

No one else can do it better

No one else can get it right

Sing your song

Morning till night

Sing it loud

Sing it out

Sing it till you're floating free

No stress nor weight touching thee

Sing for you

Sing for me

Just

Sing

68. _____

What is given is no accident
For God is not in the business of happenstance
Your life was and always has been
Meant to be
The most precious gift
Not to be spent wildly
Or left out with a reckless disregard

Life is not made up of accidents or coincidence
Reflect and you shall see
There is greatness in every life
The possibility for good and bad
The propensity for success & failure
Life is to be lived, loved, and enjoyed

Everyday isn't peachy, all skies aren't blue
But the dark days strengthen
And the good renew
Quiet days are to reflect, ready and prepare
For the life ahead and the greatness there.

Stand tall or short, thick or thin
Just be ready to show the world
The greatness growing within

And live life mightily

SECTION 7:

Challenge Quest

69. _____

A cost benefit analysis

Strangers are just easier

They are fleeting

The impressions they make

Are like sand

Judgments like new winds

Impacts like a paper cut

Quick pain

Quick heal

It's the ones who aren't so temporary

The ones whose glares linger

Those faces that hurt

With a familiarity that make one lose all clarity

It's the ones that get the keys

Even if they didn't ask

Because as extensions of yourself

There is no hesitation to access

Those are the ones

The friends & lovers

Acquaintances & brethren

They are the difficult

Because their impact is cement

Impressions are scars

And judgments like bitters famines

That make you starved for attention

Speak not of their greater benefits

For only a few possess them

So labels are given judiciously

Suspiciously

Because I know

I can't take the injury

It's sad really

To be afraid of those

Who seem to only do good to me

Whose love is like food to me

But none the less

Some build walls

While I build a fortress

A test to those & their worthiness

Protecting what's often thought to be worthless

Is it really worth this?

Cost benefit analysis

70. _____

Solitary confinement

Locked in a room with no escape

No windows only doors

Which chance do you take?

No table just keys

Spread on the floor

Always wanting to leave

While always wanting more

More time to think

To plan before acting

It's a risk to try

Comfort to wait

Wait for someone else to aid the escape

Solitary confinement

By one's own means

Though a reality

Freedom seems like a dream

Risky business this life thing

71. _____

Intelligence is not a matter of coincidence
Belligerence is a matter of ill contempt
The abstract helps to open the mind
If you have the patience and time
The imagination is abstract
It should not be constrained
Put into a bureaucracy's frame
Effective yet bland
Efficient
Wasting neither time or space
But containing neither creativity nor grace
So which do you prefer?
Abstract or bureaucracy
Free thought or an iron cage mentality
It's a query for both you and me
Do we risk it all
And think freely
Or stay in our box
A coffin to general society.

72. _____

The mind is a terrible thing to waste
To be an empty vessel
Only taking up space
The mind should be working
Ever evolving
Never contracting
Extracting beauty from the common
Decorating life with laughter
Spreading the joy of enlightenment
Never mind money or power
Getting nowhere hour by hour
Hours you can't get back
A waste you can't undo
A delicate tool often misused
And, so are you
Dwindling behind the digital façade
Wasting underneath self-constructed limitations
And imaginary inadequacy
The ball and chain of societal domains
Rest on feet and neck
As the cerebral key
Remains unnoticed and unchecked
Rusted by saline spheres
And years of neglect
As you bawl on the chain
Eyes too blurred to realize
You were long ago released
So broken by dictated burdens
You locked away the key
And let it waste
What a terrible thing to do

73. _____

Brilliant minds ramble thoughts
Daily battles fought
A piece of mind
On public display
But do the common folk
Know what has been said
Or what to say
Or is it misconstrued
Again and again
Did brilliance die in vain?
For if a tree falls and no one hears it
Does it make a sound?
Like a brilliant mind silenced too early
Were they ever around?
Was their life wasted in pain
Has ignorance taken the reigns
Is a tree left unheard
Not still a tree fallen
Or is it just the distant sound
Woven into the ground
Is a genius unknown
Still a light unbroken
Busy mind or idle display
Magnificent oak to a match stick
A fire burning in every way
Open eyes see the flame
Open ears begin to hear
Brilliant minds' rambled thoughts
A symphony of philosophy
Blazing a new way

74. _____

Natural or Synthetic
Real versus fake
Put the real under wraps
Bound in synthetic curls
Or put the natural in the rain
For a chemical burn
Is it your choice
Or the pressures of society
To be or not to be
Strike your own identity?
Or are you more than your hair
It is just the adorning piece
On a jewel too priceless
Just a part of who you are
But not your defining characteristic
I wear an afro
But that's doesn't mean I am one
I've had a perm
But never been a carbon copy
I wasn't trying to be someone else
Just exploring a different look
A different side of me
What is on the outside
Does not define the entirety
What you see is never the full story
The cover may be misleading
Because you're not used to
The presentation you are now receiving
I speak as real as I write
No matter the authenticity of my hair
Or pressure of society
I speak my truth
From root to tip
Even if the follicles split

75. _____

Paint a picture
But use no paint
Let words become the color
Complexity the ink
Cadence is your brush
Across a blank canvas
Found in the mind's eye
With precision and rhythm
And a vocabulary wide
Tell the story of a rising tide
Detail the waves as they crash and fall
Depict the foam on the ocean's floor
Submerge the mind into a world new
Explore the depths they never knew
And once they see the picture so clear
Flip it and expose the mirror
Deep in their thoughts
Brings darkness to light
Open the vault of the mind
Paint a picture
Enhance a life

76. _____

Ashes to Ashes
Dust to dust
The only way some people are hushed
The mind is wasted
The voice gone dry
The eyes are closed
Though they never saw the sky
The ocean was always too deep
The space was too much to grasp
Even simple friendships never seem to last
The desires of the mind
Reach far and wide
The storms still raged
The paradise island
A mirage that fades
Twisted reality spring to view
Helpless grasping
Thrashing against you
The waves of life
A cleansing cliché
The night gives way
And tomorrow is stuck on yesterday
Perpendicular to success
Acute disdain
Obtuse depression
A life so dreadful
Shame
Ashes to Ashes
Dust to dust
What is the difference you've made
Since your birth?

SECTION 8:

Ticks of Time

77. _____

tick tock

beat drops

fun stops

reality

begins

life lessons

set in

tables set

appetites whet

lives ended

time ongoing

laughter rolling

tears flowing

darkness rising

faded sun

growing and failing

loving and ailing

wailing women

groaning men

new days begin

sun in

night out

around the bend

joyous shouts

pain be gone

riddles and amore

faces renewed

tick tock

it won't stop

river ever flowing

never stopping

no woman no man

drip drop

hour glass

filled with the sands

of Time

78. _____

Too easy or too obvious
The big words of the little say
Say too much
When they mean so little

The microcosm of destiny
Surpasses the reality
Situations arise
Handle it wrong and demise

The imminent and prominent
Substantiate
Suffocation ensues
The life won't last
The world weighs down
Hard and fast

Living causes death
Immortality is the life you seek
But without death to look forward
Boredom will compare
What is happening here
To what happened there

The moments will pass forever and a day
Wishing and hoping
Till they all pass away
Lasting forever
Is grasping for straws

The air slips through the fingers
And babies never learn to crawl
Walking is out the question
Life is out of existence

It happened so fast
No one can resist it
The future becomes the past
Tomorrow becomes today
Hidden things become obvious
As we all pass away

79. _____

Today wasn't productive
In terms of academia
They want me to read books
On text
Listen to lectures
On end
To expand my horizons
While my brain rots on end
But today was wonderful
In the world of curiosity
I am searching myself
Exploring once hidden beliefs
Today was not lost
Because I decided that class can wait
Because I choose to create
To relate myself to someone else
To think of something new
I don't take enough time
To do what I ought to do
Time management would allow me
To do both in order and simplicity
But like time, it's management
Often runs away from me
So sometimes, I dedicate a time to me

80. _____

The trees outside

Move in the breeze

Individual leaves dance

A romance between solids and air

Blowing with grace

From here to there

Seasons glide on fresh winds

Colors swirl as a change begins

Fire spread down the lane

Golden orange and rich reds

Set the view aflame

Never does the world

Have so much color

A tapestry of foliage

Trees sway and leaves dance

Outside my windows nature occurs

New life. Old memories.

A new season to be

It sings "Let's commence"

And so, it has begun

81. _____

Sunshine and sour pops

Climbing to the tippy top

Tumble down

The well is full

The full moon glows

A mother's lullaby

Baby swings

The day begins

Repetitions causes us to

Repeat again and again

The world turns

Things change

Men to boys

Women to girls

The rhetoric of life

Roll a dice

Sound mind

Loose body

The battles between hottie or nottie

The made up and abstract

Shiny objects

Keep drivers off track

And out of the loop

Living rocks always have the scoop

Or ice cream with a cherry on top

To bottom

Tumbling down

Staring up at the sky

As the world goes

Round.... and Round....and Round...

82. _____

Dance
Lied
Sang
Lied
Woke
Cried
Walked
Silence
Talked
Empty
Rested
Never
Fell down
Light as a feather
Never Never
Say forever
It gets too long
Won't carry on
Then let down
Sunken
Sink in ground
Filled to the top
Brimming over
And under the bridge
Water trickled
Old Man Hope's
Mustache tickled

SECTION 9:

Destination: Transformation

83. _____

10 Weeks

Created hundreds of emotions

10 Weeks

Revealed my devotion

11 Weeks

Forced out the truth

It took 11 weeks for me to be

Open and honest with you

Just think of what 12 could do

When each week feels like a month

12 is a little much

A year with you

And I'd feel something new

Already, there is a better me

Because of 10 weeks with you

84. _____

Conversations of revelation

Nights of debate

Anticipating the arrival

Of new knowledge

Challenging old dogma

Teacher, teacher

I raised my hand

You answered with wisdom

And kindness too

Rescuing me from myself

Testing my notions

Side track the stubbornness

Cultivating transformation

An identify shift

Complex simplifications

Gratitude

The reoccurrence of challenge

The consistency of growth

Each conversation like

The silk of a cocoon

Energizing, refreshing

Emerging a new

85. _____

I see the change

Feel it on the inside

Knowing I can move forward

Wasn't made to stand still

Born to make moves

Change is in my blood

My uncles fought for progress

My mother creates shifts

I have a heritage of revolution

It never came easy

But good things rarely do

Can't happen while standing still

So, I fly on wings of poetry

A wordsmith of change

Manifest the inward out of me

Set to shake the world

Starting with this stage

86. _____

Her head hangs low
Thumbs to eyes
The pressure is too much
Eyes too heavy
Solitary though surrounded
Too much space for confinement
But still oppressed by the past's burdens
Her little strength is fleeting
Moments to days to weeks
But the remaining is resilient
Stubborn determination to survive
She turns her oppression
Into a weight lifting lesson
Using her baggage as dumbbells
She no long curls into to ball
But instead curls the weight
So that she can push up
From the depths of depression
Sit up when life knocks her down
And pull herself past
The prison bars on her mind
The resilient woman's workout
Transformed a warzone into a playground
She can walked with light eyes
And a head held high
She did not succumb
She fought and survived

87. _____

As time slips through clasped hands
Chaos has never been
Relegated only to theory
An all-consuming reality
Threatening remaining grains of dignity

Buried in clay walls
Reflection of earth and melanin
A unique predicament
Handled with fragile hands
Stitching together the broken remnants

Sterile love to treat the wounds
Before infection of past discolors the future
And inadequacy leaks to the surface
Sugar coated with gold plates

Bleached lessons of history
Make colors into faded stains
Tears of ancestors fall
To water next generations
Who only have umbrellas
And falsified destinations

Malnutrition of substance
Cause fruitful seeds to harden
And cake with the dust of distraction

Water from tears won't take
Spoiled grapes to the victors
A prize of disillusion
Floods the mind and opens the eyes
Hydration to the hardened
Poison to mine
As stone hearts reek of dead flesh

88. _____

Who Knew
Sitting in the clouds
Could make me so... heavy
The weight of the world
Isn't on my shoulders
But the burdens of the past
Lie strapped to my ankle
The one bracelet I would gladly lose
Won't let me break loose
Instead it drags me
From stratosphere to mantle
Hoping to bury my promise
Far beneath the gravel
As it were my resting place
Not knowing that the sunshine
Trapped in my eyes
Helps me to see through the darkness and lies
And find what lives beyond the deception
An intersection of what was and yet can be
The burdens become building blocks
Supporting my destiny and steadying my feet
This way I can build a staircase
Back to my cloud
So I'm not sitting alone,
But am enjoying the view with a crowd

89. _____

The quality of my melody

Lacks substance and harmony

It is a jail bird

Begging to be free

Release me

Create me again

I cannot revert

To before I began

The transformation has taken place

Can it not be erased?

I sing embrace

But ponder rejection

Contemplations stuck

Caught on jagged interactions

Transformations beckons

But my run falters

Stagnations pursues

Songs rise

Songs rise

Lifting the veil

Of imaginary bars

Free to live and be

Transformed

SECTION 10:

Who am I?

90. _____

My greatest fear is to live an irrelevant life.

To die without impacting the world
Without leaving a legacy
That exemplifies the love of God.

My second greatest fear is to die
Without living *beyond* my potential.

So my life goal will be to see my potential
And surpass it
To blaze a trail in the world
To live loudly
And boldly love in action
I want to live a life worth the sacrifice of Jesus
The grace of God
And the love of the Lord.

I want to live.
And I want the world to know that I lived
And I lived true

91. _____

Enter my thoughts & follow a labyrinth

                    Ever changing and evolving

Growing shorter.

                          Shrinking longer

Turn left and up

                    Rhymes around every corner

Psalms on the walls

                        Riddles line the steps

My mind is many stories tall

                          And novels deep

Oceans of introspection

          Mirrors of society's reflection

        Conundrums of philosophy and fashion

        Innovations fly like reindeer in the night

The wing of a Pegasus

                      Won't bring you to the top

Sleep only exaggerates

                          There is no stop

Step into the maze

                          To find no floor

        Do you dare even open the door?

92. _____

Think hard

Play fast

Time flies

Make it last

Wicked wonder

While good sleeps

Trickery manifest

As the meek weep

Different between night and day

Confusion lies east

West side comprehension

The night absent of color

White as the blackest day

Opposites side by side

Resting in my head

Come in and play

93. _____

I'm at my best
In the dead of the night
Peer outside
Only to be without sight
A world silent and still
My words become heinously ill
Falsified intelligence
Delicate ego management
Expulsion of contaminants
Daily remnants
Of interactions gone south
And expectations divided by reality
The war between desire and necessity
Rages quietly
Through the darkness of night
Spilling ink
Shedding lead
The bitter and broken
On display for the populace to see
Easy to digest as common rhymes
The sweet venom of a twisted mind

94. _____

I am a contradiction that needs no correcting
A living enigma that will keep you guessing
With arms for holding
And strength for standing
I have the cold that warms your heart
And the joy for your dark

Soft enough to hold
But hard enough to hold on to
I am the missing link in humanity
The complexity of simplicity
I am who He created me to be
The mountain you can't climb
The whisper you can't forget

There when you need me
But gone before you see me
And oxymoron of the highest intellect
I am the mirror that sees its reflection in you
Glass eyes and golden heart
Tears flood my soul
Though I have dry eyes

To figure me out
Is to lose yourself
To chase my dreams
You become out of breath

Close yet out of reach
Loving but hard to keep
Fleetingly permanent
Longing for home as I run away

Strong enough to love me
When the world wont
Hard enough to stand
The winds blowing my way
Soft enough to appreciate each new day

I am a soft rock
From surface to core
With feet planted firmly
And wings longing to soar

95. _____

The rabbling
The babbling
The deleted thoughts
Sound too much
Like subliminal messages
Subtweeting
Like my beak broke
Writing the ultra-vague to
Maintain an expulsion of expression
And the anonymity of ambiguity
Because out right expression
Is deemed unacceptable
Straight forward intentions
Seem unnatural
Mystery and ambiguity
The unfortunate propensity
All contradicting
My natural tendencies
So excuse me for my candor
My obvious behavior
Lying takes too much energy
Fronting is so backwards to me
Loving is most natural
Expression is deemed crucial
And interaction is principle
Call me a deviant
But I want my love
My like & my interest
To be evident

96. _____

I contemplate in poetry
Thoughts are a flow
My woes are a song

So if you see me
Mouthing rhymes to myself
I'm not singing
Just thinking

Lost in its depths
Allowing rhymes to untangle
The mental labyrinth

Because poetry
Solves my problems best
Try it for yourself & put me to the test

97. _____

Can't categorize me
No label will stick
I am sweet & sassy
Intelligent and belligerent
Loud & classy
Silly with soliloquies
Generous to most
Cheap to some
Polite to the majority
And a wrath on the run

But even then there is still
So much more
No one label
Can't tell my joys
Or expose my fears
Summarize my inquiries
Or detail insecurities
Say nothing of the abundance of confidence
The baritone laughter
Or the falsetto chatter

You may look at me

And categorize what you see

But the outside is truly skin deep

The scars tell more stories by their cells

Than those who know me well

A plethora of experience

Swirls and colors the epidermis

With a swagger only found

In an underage thermos

But my beauty and my flaws

And all the things in between

Are much more than a single faced identity

A dodecahedron doesn't have enough sides

To explain all the facets that make me

So you will definitely run out of breath

Summarizing this anthology

Into a neat square category

For categories are made to broken

And I refuse to be any kind of token

So please don't

Please don't

Limit Me

98. _____

Self-conscious
Yet unaware
From the wind up there
To the flow of my hair
I wonder what they see
Do they judge me
Why am I defensive
When no one has attacked
Why is there a barrier
Against the thin of air
Fixated on what 'they' think
Even when there is no one there
My thoughts revolve around them and me
What they see
Who am me
I mean Who and I
Who am I

The voice of society
Their toy to mold
The doors were locked
Though no one
Even bothered to knock
Shut out and shut in
Where do I begin
If only I could see
What I am saying
Who I'm becoming
She said to get a style
But I like being a chameleon
Reflecting my surroundings?
I still don't know who I am
Or what I am about
Oh but, don't worry

I will find out
I'll report my findings
At oh- two hundred o'clock
Just you watch...you watch
You watch and I wonder
What do you see
What are your thoughts
And how do they relate to me
The paranoia is real and unjust
Lust for attention
Shun from the light
It's no wonder I don't sleep at night
Frightful things that one can see
With eyes closed
In the luminesce of sleep
Explore my
Explore my mind
And what do I find
You..& you...& you... & you

But where am I
Where is the me
Lost, unfounded, uncreated, unbound
Society may have influence
But should it have the final say
I think about your response
To everything I write
On every page
Maybe I won't escape it
But I will not embrace it
Just face it head on
No mask to hide behind
I will find out who I am
And this me...
It will be mine

99. _____

I have the privilege of being black.
I have the privilege of not going to the tanning
salon to have my sun kissed skin shine like dewy
gold.
I have the privilege of not needing a perm,
because my curls were born tight.
I have the privilege of being black
I can see both sides of the fence, even if one
doesn't allow me
And one doesn't recognize me as I am.
I have the privilege of a long and complex history
that is still being understood and made.
I have the privilege to know the struggle of success
and the value of a helping hand.
I have the privilege to being an hour glass every
minute of the day.
And that my 3 syllable words and black skin with so
called white filling
Promotes a perplexity that confuses even me
I have the privilege of being a soft rock and a stone
pillow
I have the privilege to recognize privilege and irony
when I write it,

But still delight in my sun lit melanin in the colorblind
world as I step out of the lines.
I have the privilege of being both human and
African but more so American with no home to call
my own but enough shoes to build a fort.
I have the complexity of an ecosystem but am only
seen through a times 50 microscope
I see the black and the white,
but also the grey and the brown.
I have the privilege of a puffy pony tail without
humidity.
And I can laugh without humility.
But mostly, I have the privilege of knowing that
there are malleable limitations placed on my skin
that I am awarded the chance to break as I
saunter down the street in a world the ignores me
with a mesmerized gaze, jaw dropping from the
gravity of its contradictions.
Yes, I have the privilege of being black.

100. ____Epilogue_____

This is my diary
A gateway into me
My thoughts and being
The reasons to my actions
My needs and satisfactions
The distractions and rapture
Why and how I love
What I believe
And how I disagree
This is my diary,
This is me

<u>Acknowledgments</u>

A big thank you to all those who listened to a multitude of impromptu readings and encouraged me throughout the entire six year process.
Each of you helped to make this dream into a reality, thank you!

Notes

<u>Spread the Word!</u>

Have a favorite line? Is there a poem that you can't get out of your head? Maybe you made an awesome title. Well, why not share it!? Tweet it, update a status, or snap a picture to share your experience. Use the hashtag #ClichesNOtherPrettyThings to join the conversation.
Don't forget to let me know what you think
--@MissONadine

www.ingramcontent.com/pod-product-compliance
Lightning Source LLC
Chambersburg PA
CBHW071226090426
42736CB00014B/2988